THE DIGITAL NOMAD

By Harry Holland

The Complete Guide to Becoming a Digital Nomad in the 21st Century

Table of Contents

The Author

Harry Holland is a digital nomad, company director and the author of 'Digital Nomad'. Harry was born in London and has travelled to and worked in over 70 countries and is currently based in Dubai.

Harry is an experienced British digital nomad, having escaped the rat race in the City of London. With a Masters degree from King's College and over twenty years commercial and sales experience, twelve of which as CEO, Harry has a unique ability to break down and pass on the concept of the remote working lifestyle.

Prologue

"Because in the end, you won't remember the time you spent working in the office or mowing your lawn. Climb that goddamn mountain."

Jack Kerouac

The term "Digital Nomad" has been around since the beginning of the Internet. People have been using the internet, online tools, apps, and technology to escape the 9 to 5 Rat Race. This process was accelerated by the Covid pandemic and pushed people towards working remotely while companies quickly realized that productivity could be maintained (or if not increased in some cases) with their employees off-site, with no need for expensive office space.

What our parents or grandparents defined as a "job for life" in the 21st century is no longer applicable. The speed of change in society has been remarkable and now it is possible to use technology to free yourself and use the Internet to generate income in ways in which would baffle the older generation. With globalization and the growth of the internet, the world has shrunk and with your own conviction, this backdrop can become the new marketplace for a generation of digital nomads.

The book by Tim Ferris called "The Four-Hour Work Week" kickstarted the idea that there is a different way of doing things. Most people are going to be working a lot more hours than four hours a week and quite often people that work for themselves and set up businesses or even with passive income streams, probably work 40 plus hours a week.

However, by redefining the concept of work outside of the 9 to 5, it can become something a person loves, a passion, and in fact, can be all-consuming.

Equally unlike the beach and hammock cover of "The Four Hour Work Week," it's not going to be lying on a beach in Thailand forever - doing nothing. The lack of focus and of a life mission isn't necessarily going to make you happy and very often you will quickly return to the base level of happiness you had previously.

This digital nomadic lifestyle isn't about making lots of money, this is not a blueprint for a get rich quick scheme, although, money is important. However, it is more of being time rich, doing what you want to selfishly, and being your own boss, whilst having an enjoyable lifestyle.

However, if you ever find yourself wondering "What am I doing with my life?" The journey of becoming a global digital nomad and the adventure awaits…

UNPLUGGING FROM THE MATRIX

Chapter 1
Unplugging from the Matrix

"If to live in this style is to be eccentric, it must be confessed that there is something good in eccentricity."
Around the World in 80 Days - Jules Verne

The rise of social media and the wonders of technology are simply amazing certainly for people who are my age. During my childhood and my teenage years, there was no Internet, there certainly wasn't any technology like this. For most people, technology has increasingly become a vital part of life. Throughout the day, you can turn to your computers, tablets, phones, and other gadgets, whether to connect with family and friends, for work, to answer questions, handle our schedules, or offer distraction or entertainment. Our life can be encapsulated in a mobile phone – photos, videos, movies, music, productivity tools, communication, entertainment, maps, finances, games.

Indeed, it is now possible to sit in a coffee shop or on the beach and complete online work, check our finances, upload, and download to and from the cloud, speak to people on Skype, speak to family and friends and do a lot of business online with our global connectivity.

One of the most typical questions from people who are working in a conventional office environment – "the 9 to 5", is how to become a digital nomad. People see images of remote workers on social media sitting on a sunny white sand beach, laptop in hand, making an income, and wonder how they can do that too. However, remote work is not as easy as that stereotype of sitting by the pool with a laptop, while working on your tan.

It needs hard work to get the correct income stream, build a brand and even more commitment to keep it going in a steadfast way, beyond the initial enthusiasm of business creation. It's simple to skip out on work and to explore instead - escapism. That's why you need to be disciplined and focused on hitting your deadlines and remaining on track.

When discussing the digital nomad lifestyle in this book, it isn't a life coaching book, or finding your passion in a spiritual sense. This is in a concrete sense of practicality and what do you like to do? What is it that you do and have enjoyed doing since you were a child? What would you do if you were on an island for the rest of your life and you could only do one thing? What is the thing you can do to make money and hopefully enjoy your work?

It also isn't about trying to conquer the Internet and make millions because the real joy of digital nomadism is that you are freeing up time. Time is a vital commodity because you don't know how long or short your life is going to be. As corny as it sounds, it is about having no regrets "carpe diem" - seize the day.

However, truly, when you're on your death bed, you don't want to look back and think I wish I'd been to that country, I wish I'd spend more time doing this. I'm sure there are not many people that say they wish they had spent more time commuting to work and sitting in an office doing a job they don't like. Of course, work is important, and doing nothing is not recommended. A person needs projects and focus. However, this is not about working four hours a week but this is probably working 40 hours a week while you run a business and work online but it doesn't feel like work because the work often becomes your passion and you are enjoying the lifestyle and work-life balance you desired.

Be Desperate to Get Away

You may well have come across quite several people who dislike their regular jobs. However, when we hear the stories of digital nomads, we realize that they do not dislike their jobs. They truly hate their jobs. They are depressed. They are trapped and suffocated. Within all of us, there can be a feeling that you need to escape the matrix, unplugging, a sense of being a rebel and a nomad. Not doing what other people tell you. You don't have to do the 9 to 5, you don't have to wear a tie, you don't have to be in a cubicle, you don't have to get a pension when you are 68 and you can take risks because adventure without risk is impossible. These are only some ways digital nomads feel right before they leap. The extreme need to make a significant change in their lives leads them towards the nomadic lifestyle.

They are desperate for freedom which helps encourage them to do whatever it takes to succeed. It is the desperation or stimulation that pushes them to go all in. Without that need or mental impetus, you may not set yourself up for success properly. The urgent need to leave your old life behind will encourage you during the challenges you will encounter as a digital nomad.

A very important question before you sell everything, quit your job, and get on the next flight to Asia is this escapism. Are you running away or using this as a form of "self-development"? The old saying is true, the grass is always greener, If you're in an office right now, you're probably looking out of the window and dreaming about traveling to Thailand, Dubai, or Brazil to work. However, there could well be plenty of times as a digital nomad, where you dream about your home, family, and friends, going to the pub, and doing your normal daily routine activities.

Prepare for the Nomadic Lifestyle

Before you quit your average 9-5 job and pack your stuff, you need to ensure you can do this and that you're ready. When daydreaming, the nomadic lifestyle is ideal for you. It is all sunshine, rainbows, and unicorns. However, do bear in mind that many digital nomads eventually experience some form of loneliness and burnout from the nomadic lifestyle. Becoming a digital nomad is a way of living life that is completely different from others. But it is not the cure to all your worries.

You will have some awesome moments, but you will have unpleasant ones as well. That is all part of the digital nomad package.

At first, forget about visiting many different countries in a short space of time. Many digital nomads first establish a base in a country that's affordable and stay there for a few months or more. Unless you have a big amount of cash on hand, you will need to adjust your lifestyle and budget to this new way of living.

Are you planning on building your own business? Then you'll need significant sums of money to do that properly. That's true, especially if you wish to have more free time in the future. Beginner digital nomads often lodge in Airbnbs and hostels instead of renting apartments or luxurious hotels upon arrival to remain on budget and save some cash.

Practice the 4-Hour Work Week

The 4-Hour Work Week by Tim Ferries has sold more than 1.3 million copies and has been translated into thirty-five languages. It has also been a New York Times best-seller for more than four years. The main idea behind the book is to work less and make more money, just like working smarter and not harder. It's a good place to start on the Digital Nomad journey. The author mentions the need to handle your time smartly instead of fitting everything into your schedule to accomplish more to increase team motivation.

Why don't you move somewhere in the world that is cheaper to live in, has a better climate? Bring your computer and work remotely whenever you want. That is the crux of the 4-Hour Work Week. The whole idea revolving around the 4-hour workweek emphasizes that people have enough time. We simply do not know how to handle it efficiently. In short, there is no such thing as "too little time" or "too busy."

Pursue your passion

How many people have regular jobs that they truly enjoy? Many come to dread Monday mornings and the alarm call. Working thirty-five to forty hours per week, jumping from one payday to the other in many developed countries has become the norm. Tim Ferris recommends breaking that norm. He encourages you to look deep within yourself and embrace your entrepreneurial instincts. Sit back and assess what you like to do in your life. Find your passion and go for it. That tip is useful for individuals wanting to break the shackles of corporate slavery and run their own businesses.

Use the 80/20 principle

Tim Ferris also recommends finding twenty percent of the work that draws eighty percent of your productivity and leaves the rest. In short, eighty percent of your business's income comes from twenty percent of customers. That's what you need to determine and focus on.

Automate and delegate your tasks

Ferris also explained reasons not to automate something that can be eliminated and not delegate something that can be streamlined or automated. Another idea the 4-Hour Work Week teaches you is to begin outsourcing your work. If there is a task that somebody else could do for you, wait no longer and delegate it right away.

Create a to-do and not-to-do list

We often create a to-do list and outline the things we need to do. However, your list is composed of things that don't need your attention half of the time. The idea of delegation fits here perfectly. Create a list of everything you can delegate to somebody else so you can divert your attention towards more essential tasks for the day or the week ahead.

Evaluate Yourself

The goal of 'unplugging from the Matrix' is to help you realize whether the nomadic lifestyle is suitable for you. It will help you understand whether you like to be a digital nomad or the perfect time for you to find a new job. Try to work as a digital nomad for a few weeks and take note of how you feel. Do you wish to do it again? Were there any things you wanted to be better ready for first? Or did you feel like it was not for you?

Remember that trial runs do not often provide an exact representation of what it will be like. There will be some awesome epiphanies and life experiences you simply cannot get in two weeks. Nonetheless, there will be other unforeseen and sometimes unsettling challenges that happen over long-term periods too.

Chapter 2
Adventure or Escapism

"He was mastered by the sheer surging of life, the tidal wave of being"
Jack London

The transition from a full-time job to a digital nomad or location-independent work is exciting. However, as with any lifestyle change, you will need to plan and make necessary adjustments to prevent unwanted stress and from feeling overwhelmed.

For some, changeover fits their personality easily, while others find it more complicated and challenging.

The Unbearable Lightness of Being

How do we view life? An essential philosophical question at the heart of digital nomadism, perhaps a question that arises at the dark hour in the middle of the night. Should a digital nomad take life seriously or not?

Should we consider our digital nomad life as heavy or light? Should a digital nomad not take life too seriously (the light), enjoy all the pleasures a remote existence affords, and reject all heavier philosophy of life and the weight of responsibilities? These are the fundamental question posed by Milan Kundera at the heart of his novel "The Unbearable Lightness of Being" and is part of Nietzsche's idea of "eternal recurrence." The title comes from the dilemma of lightness versus gravitas.

Lightness is the idea that in our lives nothing really matters, it's all transient and the weightiness comes from the fact that we are all going to die. So, nothing matters, or does everything matter?

"The heaviest of burdens is therefore simultaneously an image of life's most intense fulfillment. The heavier the burden, the closer our

lives come to the earth, the more real and truthful they become. Conversely, the absolute absence of burden causes man to be lighter than air, to soar into heights, take leave of the earth and his earthly being, and become only half real, his movements as free as they are insignificant. What then shall we choose? Weight or lightness?"
Milan Kundera, The Unbearable Lightness of Being

Should you be free like a sailor on the high seas or do you bring your boat into the harbor to dock and walk on dry land. The digital nomad lifestyle is very attractive because you've got a lot of time for yourself, you can travel and have adventures whilst still working and earning an income.

Do we want to make our mark on the world and not to go "gentle into that good night" as in the poem by Dylan Thomas? There is no correct answer to this fundamental philosophical question as it is a personal, subjective decision and a reason for the onset of this journey onwards to a new lifestyle.

Another classic text to read when considering your future as a nomad is "How I Found Freedom in an Unfree World" by Harry Browne, first published in 1973. In the book is the idea that a person's happiness is the highest goal that can be achieved in life. That freedom comes from living your life as you see fit – as in the link to digital nomadism. Happiness and freedom are very feasible and it's never too late to change your life.

The Journey to a New Lifestyle

An aspiring digital nomad does not wake up and catch a flight without any plan. Such spontaneity does not usually take place, as there are many things involved along the way. Like your normal life, failing to plan as a digital nomad only sets you up for failure. When traveling you could find a lot of people that are escaping from their home country because they don't like it or something has happened in their lives. Basically, they are running away from something and hoping to find happiness through a more hedonistic lifestyle. They find a new destination and so they just pack up everything and off they go. Often nomads carry a feeling of guilt, dependent on their own self-discipline and work ethic, as they are working less hours as in a more ideal environment.

Certainly, when traveling, people will return more open-minded, with new experiences to bring back to their life or their jobs, their health, their 'look', their skills or they've changed their relationships. Traveling has positively impacted their lives.

Even though the four-hour workweek and digital nomad model suggests that it is all like lying in the hammock, working four hours a day, the reality often is that you are going to take your problems with you. So, if you're stressed, feeling low, and unhappy in your home country then those issues are likely to surface eventually whilst in a new location. However, if you are happy and content, good at self-discipline and routines, good social skills then you will also take that with you. Accept that you are the common denominator wherever you go.

Before setting off, you must understand when and how to get there. That suggests that you have a plan you need to achieve in the end. Consider the smaller details as that is what determines your ultimate success.

Cut unnecessary expenses

Most importantly, make sure you have taken proper care of your insurance and health. To actualize your dreams of becoming a digital nomad, you should cut down on your expenses because you'll need savings to account for your emergency and financial needs while away.

Try to get rid of unnecessary budgets like paid memberships or gym subscriptions. Likewise, you can sell unused items in your garage so that you don't need to pay for storage costs. When you sort such basic needs, your life as a digital nomad takes a reality route through embracing some element of minimalism.

Embrace your new life

There may be instances when you question your decision to leave your full-time career or job but take note that this is a fresh start. Most likely you've got a job or you're doing something right now which is ticking along, it's paying the bills. It might be a bit mundane, in an office or a supermarket. At the same time, it is possible to set something up online in the evenings and on the weekends. A small online business, a little niche that will eventually allow you to quit that primary job.

You can always get another job in the future if things do not work out. But first, you should embrace the changes and offer your new life everything you've got. Businesses could take time to set up and moving around or remote living could have inherent challenges as with any other kind of lifestyle.

You may likely want to become a digital nomad as you love many aspects of this lifestyle, such as flexibility and freedom. Thus, do not let those challenges overwhelm you.

With some adjustments and preparations, you can have a smooth transition from your full-time job to becoming a digital nomad.

Another important detail is to familiarise yourself with the language you will use to communicate with foreigners. Understanding their local dialect also helps in understanding the local culture more easily.

Choose where you like to go in the future and plan for it

Apart from finances, consider your new business or work requirements when picking destinations. Are you a creative professional? Then you may wish to be in environments that facilitate such work. Perhaps you like a place along with other digital nomads, such as a co-working space.

When searching for an online role, a good technique is trying to find a niche. Remember that you don't need to sell to every human being on the planet, you only need to sell to a very small percentage of people on the Internet. So that's finding a niche based on what you're good at, whether graphics, coding, designing, fitness, accountancy, law, or even teaching. There often will be a skillset from your childhood or a hobby or something that you're naturally good at.

Research all your needs and requirements, from the weather to the internet connection quality, co-working spaces, healthcare facilities, and more.

All places have their own surprises, but researching ahead and doing some internet research, will limit your frustrations and allow a more stress-free transition to a new lifestyle.

You could consider using co-working spaces to guarantee a flawless transition from your old office setting, particularly if you enjoyed having other colleagues around.

A few transitions straight from a corporate office to the extreme of van life and working in a coffee shop could pose many challenges but the growth of co-working spaces is the new middle ground for many.

How to Find Work Options as Digital Nomad

Before you begin seeking digital nomad jobs, you need to determine how to make money online. By that, I mean:
- Do you prefer to work as a freelancer?
- Do you like to work as a remote employee?
- Maybe you like to start your own business?

You must identify the type of remote job you prefer (if you do not like to start your own business). As mentioned above, perhaps you already have the skills and experience in your aspired job or you need help to figure out what you like, online courses can help you understand what it takes to do the job.

Probably you will be searching for entry-level remote jobs, where you could learn as you go.

Ensure that you know what you can offer to make an income online before you begin your digital nomad journey. If you do not know what you are searching for, it will be more difficult to find it. But in case you know what type of remote job you seek, then it is time to find it.

Talk to your employer

An obvious place to start looking for remote jobs is with your existing employer. Ask them whether they would be open to you working remotely. If you're working for a multinational organization, you could research whether there are any openings in other countries. Ask yourself these questions:

- Can most of the tasks you do now be done on a laptop or computer?
- Can most of the conversations or meetings with your supervisors and team members be made over the phone or online?

If yes, then talk to your employer. Check if there's any way you can change your office job to a remote job. Sometimes, organizations are very willing to cooperate rather than let you find a replacement, particularly after the lockdowns of the Covid pandemic, when the 'new normal' become normal.

It might not be full-time at the start, you can begin with a few days a week to get trust and show that you can work from home (or wherever). You could consider taking a sabbatical or requesting working on an oil rig style rota – work on – work off, a month or months at a time.

Online and remote jobs

There are various places you can turn to look for work online as a digital nomad. You can try taking on remote jobs while working as a freelancer and traveling the world. Many online remote job sites and apps such as Fiverr, We Work Remotely, FlexJobs, and UpWork post thousands of remote work jobs, as the 'Gig Economy' expands – catering for freelances and more temporary contracts and work. Many countries, such as Estonia, Malta, and Croatia provide digital nomad visas that make it simpler to navigate the legalities of working from abroad.

Furthermore, you could network globally to find work in various countries using Linkedin or Instagram, or other social media platforms.

Getting internationally recognized skills or high-in-demand qualifications in other countries could help you make you more employable.

Networking

Networking is surely one of the best ways to look for jobs, whatever type of job it may be. You can take advantage of LinkedIn and check your contacts. Anyone working in your industry might be able to connect you with someone interesting.

Try to reach out to selected former employers, team members, or classmates directly. If you had a good experience with the company, they might recall your excellent teamwork and expertise. If you're fortunate, they might need someone like you. If not, they might connect you to others and suggest you. You never know what may happen, but keep in mind that networking could bring you some amazing digital nomad jobs.

You can talk to other digital nomads (if you know any) before embarking on your journey. You can also join the digital nomad groups and forums on social media, Reddit, and online to learn from other people's experiences. You may have unique experiences, but it is always good to know beforehand. You may find yourself working in somewhat different places from what you are used to regarding lifestyle, the languages people speak, and their culture. Give yourself enough time to settle in and embrace places.

The benefit of becoming a digital nomad is that if you don't like a place you are in, you can always go somewhere else (unless there is another pandemic, of course!).

Chapter 3
Cutting the Cord

"Let us toast to animal pleasures, to escapism, to rain on the roof and instant coffee, to unemployment insurance and library cards, to absinthe and good-hearted landlords, to music and warm bodies and contraceptives... and to the "good life", whatever it is and wherever it happens to be."

Hunter S. Thompson

Digital nomads fly across the globe doing their online jobs wherever they can find a decent internet connection and a lifestyle that suits them at a cost-effective price. It remains an enviable lifestyle, but the global coronavirus pandemic made it less straightforward for some time.

Nonetheless, with borders reopening and flights taking off again, the dream of becoming a digital nomad is truly alive once more. In fact, many people have taken their work online to comply with the physical distancing recommendations. The lockdown has accelerated already existing trends and the digital nomad dream has become tangible for many, seeing that they could feasibly continue doing that in the near future. Stereotypically close to a tropical beach and at a lower cost of living.

Digital Nomads have boomed as millions of people worked remotely

According to a study from MBO Partners, 7.3 million Americans in 2019 were identified as digital nomads. Between that year and 2020, that figure increased by a staggering forty-nine percent due to the coronavirus pandemic. Today, it is estimated that there are more than 10.9 million digital nomads from America alone (MBO Partners)

The reasons behind the growth

A 'perfect storm,' is a combination of the growth of the internet and associated apps, perception of freedom, higher salary expectations, increased flexibility, and the ability to work anywhere in the globe. Besides, the lockdown from 2020 and the instruction from employers to stay away from the office. The digital nomad growth doesn't look like slowing down.
The founder of the popular website, NomadList, Pieter Levels, predicts a billion digital nomads worldwide by 2035.

Researchers have also found out that women are leading the way with digital nomadism and the increased flexibility offered has suited many women looking to start a family. In the past, becoming a mother has been a major challenge for women who wish to further their careers. Raising children and taking time off work means fewer promotions and contributes to the gender wage gap.

However, becoming a digital nomad has changed this dynamic. A release from the office desk and the 9 to 5 routine, women and other working mums have thrived in this environment, combining their work with family life. Nearly thirty percent of remote companies have female presidents, founders, or CEOs. Compared to the 5.2 percent of female CEOs in the typical workplace generally. With these statistics, it is no surprise that women prefer the nomadic lifestyle.

Remote Workers are Scattered Across the Globe

Digital nomad trends in 2021 demonstrate that the nomad population is quite mixed by nationality and comes from all corners of the globe. Among the American population, seventy percent of the digital nomads are white, fourteen percent are African American, seven percent are Asian, seven percent are Hispanic, and two percent are of other ethnicities.

Furthermore, digital nomads represent each group from seventeen to sixty-five years old and older. Contrary to stereotypes, research also shows that digital nomads are not only freelancers. They also include teachers, programmers, writers, artists, CEOs, and the list goes on. Research also shows that thirty-six percent of digital nomads freelance for different companies or through different platforms and not just solely for one.

The travel and hospitality industry is another sector where people are taking the leap into the digital nomad trend.

A report published by Airbnb in May 2021 revealed that the number of long-term stays has nearly doubled year-on-year. The size of Airbnb guest reviews citing remote work has also increased by 520 percent worldwide during that time. Fifty-five percent of long-term stay bookers surveyed in 2021 mentioned working or studying during their stay.

Airbnb foresees that most people might not continue to work only from home as we emerge from lockdowns but will look to suburban homes outside the city, forest cabins, and beach cottages for a change of scene and work productively.

What workplaces will look like post-COVID

The post-pandemic situation isn't clear yet and indeed at the time of writing the Pandemic is not truly over. However, some trends have started emerging while others have become more and more prominent.

The digital nomad lifestyle was gaining steam pre-COVID and Covid has proved to be the 'locomotive of change'. Still, more organizations are now considering the potential of long-term remote work and even questioning the need to return to a conventional office space at all, given the expense of the real estate.

Changes in communication

The unprecedented worldwide reach of the coronavirus created a substantial shift in how business owners handled their teams, upheld their business models with remote working, and how professional development and training are done. Furthermore, there has been massive growth in the use of online communication apps and video conferencing platforms such as Zoom and Microsoft Teams. With that growth, it has become even clearer that digital nomads can be as connected and efficient working remotely as they would in an in-person setting.

More people will work remotely

Organizations and businesses worldwide are continuing to explore the benefits of working remotely, including enhanced autonomy for their teams and lower operational expenses, which also often means higher job satisfaction. It looks like this way of working will be here to stay for many years.

Distributed teams are now considered a long-term opportunity instead of a short-term solution. For most digital nomads, that could indicate added job openings in the future or the possibility for more flexible current jobs to accommodate the nomadic lifestyle.

Healthcare will be more crucial than ever

With the COVID-19 putting greater pressure on healthcare systems globally, most predictions claim that general wellbeing, safety, and health will become a more important concern for digital nomads than ever before.

Most travelers purchase insurance or international coverage before leaving their home countries, this is often due to the bank or card membership that offers such protection. However, not everybody living and embarking on the nomadic lifestyle is this organized and has looked into the options of healthcare.

With the uncertainty created by the pandemic residual, they'll need to examine the present case numbers in the country, immigration requirements in terms of PCR testing and vaccination, the nearest hospitals covered in their plans, and any other local restrictions and mandates.

Flying will be more expensive and challenging.

Part of the appeal of becoming a digital nomad is saving money. If you are one, you can get some substantial tax benefits. For example, if you live in America and out of the country for 330 out of 365 days, you may qualify for the Foreign Income Exclusion Tax.

That indicates that most teleworkers reap massive benefits from being out of the nation for a longer period. Other nations have similar tax benefits too.

Nonetheless, as airlines struggle to stay afloat, the cost of flying has risen while schedules have lowered. It is safe to predict that the aviation sector will not recover for several months or even years after the pandemic. This is still unknown territory and is difficult to predict as the numbers of flights have now increased, and airports are seeing much more traffic.

Other factors will affect the destinations digital nomads pick as temporary or more permanent home bases. If you're not in the position to pack your bags and leave right away, there are other things you can do to make the entire situation easier to deal with. For instance, you can have a 'taster' by planning a vacation closer to home.

With the current challenges of air travel overseas, it might be the ideal time to get in your car and go somewhere a bit closer to home. Furthermore, traveling domestically means you can support local economies that have experienced the weight of the coronavirus pandemic, while possibly exploring a few hidden gems along the way.

The New Normal

With Covid-19 facilitating a massive shift towards remote work, the digital nomad phenomenon is set for constant expansion in the next few years. More and more companies offload costly office space, and employers and employees alike become more familiar with working remotely.

This trend was growing even before the pandemic, facilitated by the increase of co-working spaces and the establishment of digital nomad-oriented organizations. As borders slowly open and travel resumes, more and more emerging markets will look to capitalize on the growing trend of digital nomads seeking appealing, reliable, and affordable places from which to work.

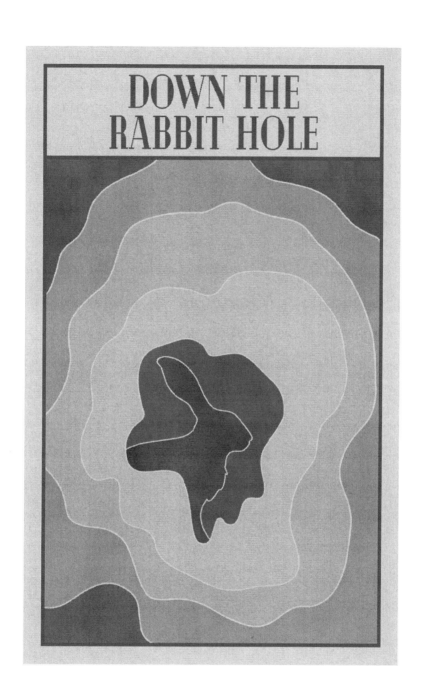

DOWN THE RABBIT HOLE

Chapter 4
Down the Rabbit Hole

One day a young Buddhist on his journey home came to the banks of a wide. He saw a great teacher on the other side of the river. The young Buddhist yells over to the teacher, "Oh wise one, can you tell me how to get to the other side of this river"?

The teacher replied, "My son, you are on the other side."
Buddhist Story

Traveling the world while working online from your computer has been a dream of many people. Nonetheless, working from foreign nations while traveling on a tourist visa is illegal in many places. In many countries, visas often expire after thirty to ninety days, and it is not always a simple process to renew them. What if you wish to stay a little bit longer? Previously it has been common for digital nomads to do 'visa runs', going to another country, crossing a border, to renew the visa of the country that they wish to stay in.

Visas and borders have not stopped digital nomads from working while traveling. But it can also make things more challenging. With travel restrictions due to the coronavirus pandemic, it has become more complicated to travel and work internationally.

Visa laws in many nations aren't set up to facilitate this new group of modern nomads who are working remotely and living around the world. Fortunately, it seems that this is starting to change. Some nations, such as Estonia (the first), some of the Caribbean islands, Mauritius, Dubai, Taiwan, Malta, Georgia, and Iceland, amongst others, have acknowledged the need for so-called *freelancer visas, remote work visas,* or *digital nomad visas* to appeal to foreigners wanting to work and contribute to their economies.

Most of these places are hoping the remote work visas will produce income to help make up for lost tourism income because of the pandemic.

Cost-Effective Places to Live for Digital Nomads

Here are some of the examples of places to work and live as digital nomads. This list also includes countries incentivizing immigration.

- ## Spain

Spain offers a non-lucrative visa allowing immigrants to stay in the country for <u>approximately a year</u>, with the ability to renew. The country is a favorite for travelers with most location independent people and it offers low-cost living and a relaxed lifestyle, mountains, and beaches. Nonetheless, technically you're not allowed to *work* on that visa. They are seeking people who are self-sufficient and retired.

- ## Norway

Norway has been in the news these days, deemed as a Scandinavian paradise with its powerful social democratic system, progressive population, natural beauty, and health. Many foreign remote workers and digital nomads would jump at the opportunity to move to this country. For up to two years, they can do that with the country's "Independent Contractor Visa".

- ## Mauritius

Mauritius is an island nation that has recently announced its special visa for remote workers. It is a beautiful nation, along with thick jungle, crystal clear water, and epic mountain peaks to climb. To be eligible for their 1-year long and free <u>Premium Visa</u>, you must make proof of your long-term stay plans and enough health and travel insurance throughout your stay.

- ## Iceland

Iceland also has its <u>long-term visa</u> for digital nomads and remote workers. The long-term visa is good for only six months for non-EU/EEA residents. Thus, it is one of the shortest digital nomads visas you can consider. However, it will be valid for ninety days if you apply while already in the European Schengen Area.

• Georgia

Georgia is one of the newest nations to provide a digital nomad referred to as <u>Remotely from Georgia</u> to help advance its economy. So, if you are a digital nomad or a remote worker, Georgia is the perfect place for you. It boasts a low cost of living, epic mountain landscapes, and vibrant cities.

• Mexico

Mexico is another hotspot for digital nomads, partly because of their long six-month tourist visa. Nonetheless, they also provide a <u>Temporary Resident Visa</u>, which is valid for a year with the ability to renew for another three years.

You must present documents verifying that you had a monthly revenue of at least $1,620 over the past six months or a bank account balance of $27,000. It's worth mentioning that the country is open to providing temporary residency to self-sufficient remote workers.

• Malta

Malta has developed its <u>Digital Nomad Residence Permit</u> targeting remote workers outside the European Union. This place has been appealing to many digital nomads for years now because of its strong internet infrastructure, widely spoken English people, and sunny island lifestyle.

It is situated near mainland Europe, the Middle East, and North Africa. That only indicates numerous opportunities for travel lovers to get out and discover nearby.

• Bali

This list will not be complete without mentioning Bali. The amazing island of Bali, Indonesia, has long been famous for digital nomads to stay. The island has recently announced that they plan to implement a <u>new digital nomad visa</u> soon.

Their remote work visa is valid for at least five years, and visa holders would not have to pay taxes on any income gained outside Bali.

- **Bermuda**

Bermuda finally joined the remote work visa club after releasing their Work From Bermuda visa to expand their old residency program that enables remote workers and digital nomads to stay in the nation for at least a year.

This visa is intended for people working from home. Bermuda hopes the new visa policy will entice long-term travelers to base on the island.

- **Antigua and Barbuda**

Recently, the Caribbean Island nation of Antigua and Barbuda announced a digital nomad visa referred to as the Nomad Digital Residence. The visa is intended for remote workers who can demonstrate the means to support themselves and any family members joining them.

The visa is applicable for two years only, and visitors are obliged to keep their health insurance plan while staying within the nation and enjoying its different beaches.

- **Barbados**

This country also opened its borders to remote workers and digital nomads seeking to escape the pandemic while residing in a wonderful island destination. Barbados offers the Barbados Welcome Stamp, a 12-month visa for remote workers which can also be renewed for even longer.

- **Cayman Islands**

The Cayman Islands also launched a special visa for digital nomads. They call the visa the Global Citizen Certificate that enables travelers to stay in the islands for at least two years. However, the income requirements for this visa are a lot steeper than other nations on this list. They mandate travelers to present an annual salary of approximately $100,000 or $150,000 for couples.

- **Costa Rica**

Many digital nomads prefer to base themselves in this country because of the laid-back lifestyle, beautiful beaches, excellent surfing, and diverse jungle, waterfalls, and volcanoes.

Currently, the country has a freelancer visa called the *Rentista*. It enables foreigners to stay at least two years with the ability to extend it. It is often utilized by retirees with a fixed income and a few entrepreneurs. You cannot be an employee for another organization on this visa.

In August 2021, the government made a special 1-year Digital Nomad Visa, which could be extended for another year. Visa holders are exempted from local income taxes, open bank accounts, and drive in the country using their own country's license.

Picking a country to live and work as a digital nomad is a challenge. While most online guides offer a decent overview of the key pros and cons, the only way to make a smart choice is to experience the place physically. The list above only includes places with digital nomad-friendly visa regimes and the list is ever-growing.

You can reside in these places for a few months or a year before making any long-term decisions.

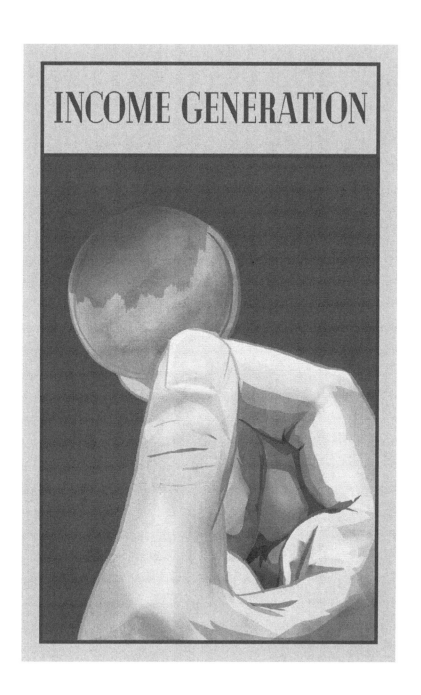

INCOME GENERATION

Chapter 5
Income Generation

"Once you decide on your occupation...you must immerse yourself in your work."

Jiro Dreams of Sushi

Digital nomads are used to working remotely from the places they travel to explore. That kind of bucket-list travel and adventurous endeavor can be a rewarding and life-changing experience. However, it can also be hard on the wallet. You need to think about jobs that you can take during your travels and be sure it won't affect the job you've got now, and you can save up money. Be sure the job you take during your travels can be done on your laptop so it's worth sitting down and considering how it could fit. I'm going to give you some tips.

You can find different ways to cut down on traveling expenses as a digital nomad. Your income is what can make or break your lifestyle. Here are practical ways to earn extra cash to keep your adventures going. There are various ways to create income as a digital nomad in countries you travel to (whether permanent or temporary, ad hoc work (such as freelancing), or by creating a Passive Income. You can start some of these in the evenings, on the weekends and in your free time whilst you are still in your traditional '9-5' job.

During your spare time, you can build a business or an online presence and that might need to do with your passion, your skillset, or simply a business/sales opportunity online. The number of possibilities is endless from teaching English online to being a professional poker player online to managing a portfolio of properties. Here are some examples to fire your imagination:

• Teaching/Tutoring

Teaching around the world has long been a popular option, both teaching English or as a qualified School teacher working in International Schools. Additionally, with the internet, there will also be a niche market, where you can teach any subject online, whether live or a recorded class to be shown on Youtube Channel. It could be a skill (such as a game or instrument) and you might teach people after your regular job in person one on one or in small groups.

One excellent way to do that is to develop an online course. Are you skilled in a specific area? You can make an online course out of it.

First, you should find a niche audience and present how your course could get them real results and help them solve an issue or problem. Popular online course topics are programming, web design, and time management.

YouTube is a good platform for tutorials, it is another perfect opportunity for making money as a digital nomad.

All you need is a laptop, a secure Wi-Fi connection. However, this is more labor-intensive as you will need to tutor students to earn extra cash.

Slowly over time, you'll be perceived as an authority in this as you're giving value to others, you are passing on knowledge. The most important thing is the perception people have of you as an authority figure as a teacher on the internet. This could be backed up with video products or by writing an online kindle or a PDF, which you can send out for marketing reasons. Eventually, you might even write a paperback or hardback book!

There is always a high demand for teaching and tutoring. You don't need to think about having a way to make money. Since you can easily work from your laptop, you can work anywhere, whether from a café, hostel, or Airbnb. This is suitable for nomads who excelled in a particular area in school or have a particular skill.

For example, Maths is a popular high-demand subject that often requires tutoring sessions for students. If you are good at mathematics, you will have no problem finding your clients. Learning a language such as English (TEFL – Teaching English as a Foreign Language) is a popular option too.

- **Freelancing**

Freelancing is another good option for remote work. Are you planning to work as a freelancer? Then certain platforms such as Fiverr for freelancing jobs might be a good idea to further explore.

All you need to do is register, make your profile stand out with all your skills and experiences listed and apply for open job positions, or clients can find you and book your services. Many jobs are available, so you have a good selection to choose from. Also, they are quite safe, as such platforms verify payment methods. You can check previous reviews to check if the client is reliable.

It is typical to see writing as a hobby or gig, not an actual job. That's why companies are paying on a per-number-of-words or a per-article basis instead of hiring actual writers to do the task. If you are good with words, know your grammar, and have excellent typing speed skills, freelancing might be the thing for you. Freelance writing or blogging is a good way to supplement your blog income.

With more publications moving online, there are many opportunities to earn a living while doing freelance gigs. Furthermore, news outlets might pay for well-written content.

Opting for a freelancing job may sound simple, but the competition is huge. You might want to set your prices as low as $4 per hour, so you can establish your reputation first to potential clients to convince the client you are worth the extra money when you deliver high quality.

Developing your Business and Brand

Starting an online business is another common way to earn income as a digital nomad. Many digital nomads started their online business while taking the year to save. By the time they venture out, they have a decent-sized customer base who will continue buying their products.

Shopify is a good option to create your website. Building your online store means you will have total control over the navigation and design of your website. You can be as creative and imaginative as you wish and profit from it. You can employ freelancers from sites like Fiverr to help you design your logo, brand, and website. When looking for freelancers to help develop your brand, try to look for the middle ground in terms of cost, so for example, designers and coders from places like Middle Europe, Poland, Hungary, Serbia, Czech Republic, etc are perfect for you. If you are looking for cheaper freelancers, the results can be a little hit and miss.

A classic text when considering developing a business and your brand is "The psychology of Persuasion" by Professor Robert Cialdini and the underlying six principles and how they help generate an income, which I will briefly summarise here. Whether your business is in an office, meeting your client or you are working on the Internet, the same principle of persuasion is needed to convince others to buy your product or service.

Listed below are steps to help get more sales or for a client to order your services.

- Liking
- Authority
- Scarcity
- Commitment/consistency
- Social proof
- Reciprocity

- Firstly, is likeability – You should get your customers to like you.

- The second principle is that you need to be authoritative, you need to be "the leader", so when customers look to your brand, they will respect and trust you, which will prompt them to follow you (for example through social media) as a trustworthy brand.

- Scarcity is the third key principle, so the "going gone..last day of the sale" last item in the showroom. Ultimately, rather than you chasing customers, they should be chasing you. It's a quirk of human psychology trick that when you see other people doing something, you trust that decision, so you go along with it. In sales, other customers will trust you because you've already got a good customer base – you have social proof through existing customers.

- When you have a good brand and are well known, customers will trust you. Generally, we all follow patterns in our lives and our decision-making.

- Commitment and Consistency is the next Principle.

- Finally, reciprocity, a common sales technique, when you get a gift or free sample, again human psychology, you will want to repay the freebie by buying that product. For example, when you get a little free taster in the supermarket, you will eventually buy the product.

There is often a ratio of "9 to 1", so for every ten pieces of information you put out there whether a video, podcast, email, or blog article for your client base, nine of those should be free to give free value to your clients.

After all this information is given out, a customer or client may well consider your authority on a topic or subject (related to your business) and you can build loyalty with your customer base through your freebies. Often a customer might sign up and buy a product, just to say thanks for that free content and information.

As a small start-up, using this form of content marketing is often effective, particularly when you have developed a brand and a unique selling point (USP). If you're focused on content quality and providing value to your niche market, people are likely to buy it.

Website

When developing your business, a good website is invaluable, you can as well use existing platforms such as Amazon, eBay, and Kindle. Again, freelancers can help in this process, although website templates can offer a cheaper do-it-yourself alternative.

Blogging

Blogging is one of the most accessible and best options to make money online. It is an excellent way to make passive income. Of course, you will need to create content regularly to add to your site and develop the website itself (as above).

Nonetheless, you can only earn income when you generate more traffic to your website. You don't need to engage with customers, have a store, or sell any products.

Instead, you can make money as you travel and sleep. How amazing is that? But how can you do this?

There are some ways to monetize your blog. One way is to find companies that will market their product on your blog. The more visitors that see and click your ads, the more money you make. Another way is becoming an affiliate and linking the affiliate link on your site.

You will receive a percentage of the sale whenever someone clicks on that link and makes a purchase through it. It's straightforward, right? But it will require some patience as your website visitors grow.

Still, it is a good option that needs less effort and enables you to devote more time to other forms of income-generating business.

Investing

Some (maybe many) digital nomads would rather not work while exploring the world. When they finally arrive at their destination, they would rather enjoy and sightsee what the place has to offer without being stuck in a co-working space or coffee shop. That suggests they need to have a decent source of passive income.

However, it is still important to have a mission/goal when setting out your plan of digital nomadism even with streams of passive income.

Many passive income sources need a huge amount of work upfront, except for investing. Investing money means your money works for you than the other way around. Clearly, you will need capital to start this process.

These days, a very common form of investing for digital nomads is through cryptocurrency or through buying shares in the stock market. Both are far more accessible in the 21st Century and no longer need to work through a stockbroker. The Covid pandemic saw the rise of the armchair investor.

A few high returns from investments coming in will help pay for a reasonable passive income as a digital nomad. Standard investments often pay out a return much more than a savings account, although there is a greater risk of your investment going down. To make enough from that travel and have all your bills paid needs a significant amount of capital to work effectively.

Thus, investing in cryptocurrency or stocks could create income, whether you look at day trading – buying and selling each day or look to hold investments for the long run. Of course, that could happen in the best-case scenario. Don't forget that there's a major risk of losing money with crypto or investments.

Crypto, in particular, is quite volatile in the short term but products such as exchange-traded funds (ETFs) are another type of investment that tracks a range of products that can offer a safer haven for investments but there is still a risk.

Nevertheless, the major advantage is that it is very accessible with the right apps on your mobile phone. After you learn how to invest in shares or crypto, you can find many opportunities with lesser-known types of investments, like other cryptocurrencies.

Another aspect of investments is that your money can be converted into cash in your account with low fees no matter where you are. That offers you immediate access to your money globally, enabling maximum flexibility.

Affiliate Marketing

Another passive way to make money as a digital nomad is through affiliate marketing. I have briefly discussed it earlier under blogging. Affiliate marketing is a system in which you create websites such as blogs that market-specific services or products. When people use the links given in the articles, they get a commission.

It does take a huge amount of work upfront and should be maintained over time. Nonetheless, there's a huge amount of flexibility when you do this for a living. You are not trading time for money, as orders can take place any time of the day. That enables you to travel, sightsee and work whenever you wish. There's also no schedule to be adhered to. Just keep in mind that it takes time to make a full-time living from this type of marketing. Thus, you must create and establish your website, social media and your brand before heading out on the road.

Rent Out Your Space, Car, or Home

Do you own a home or a car? You can earn some cash by renting out space. You can efficiently rent out your space through platforms like Airbnb. Depending on the size of your property, you can rent out the entire space at once, or you can rent out different bedrooms for multiple people. It can even be possible to sub-let property if allowed to do so.

Moreover, you can rent out your car through car-sharing platforms such as <u>Getaround</u>. Other applications let you rent out your garage, parking space, or storage space.

You need to be a bit creative to facilitate these rentals remotely. For instance, you can install a digital keypad or digital locks for your home.

Writing a Book

Another way to make passive income is by writing and publishing an eBook. Freelancers can also assist in the process of writing and producing a Kindle book.

It would have been a long and challenging process writing a book in times past, involving working with agents and publishers, possibly getting rejected, and even if it got published you would be receiving just a tiny cut of the royalties. Writing a book needs time and a routine. It can be challenging at first but can quickly become immersive.

You can start by simply writing a book in a Word document. You get somebody to check, you can give your friend or you can pay somebody (freelancer) to do the copy/line editing and the graphic designs, including a front cover. In the beginning, you may think that you do not actually have that much to say about a subject or there are so many other books and manuals out there already. Researching on a topic can help here and even finding a writer to put your prose into a document that is readable and flows – for example, you can use the service of a ghostwriter.

Sell Your Photo and Video Content

One of the benefits of being a traveler is seeing a plethora of scenic views. Buy yourself a high-quality camera and take quality photos and videos. You can sell them online and make money.

Different types of companies and businesses are looking for original photos and videos to use in their campaigns. Who knows? You might make a decent living out of selling stock materials.

You see, the sky is the limit when we talk about making money online as a digital nomad. My list is by no means comprehensive but offers you a glimpse of what's possible. Full-time living can be made online with determination and persistence, allowing you to travel the world simultaneously.

LIVING COSTS

Chapter 6
The Road is Life

"Be the flame, not the moth."
Casanova

Becoming a digital nomad indicates having the freedom to pursue a career without being tied down to your desks. Digital nomads include employees, independent contractors, and freelancers who prefer remote work to an office cubicle.

There are a few vital financial considerations to weigh in the balance, especially if you live on the road full-time or close to it, using a time on–time off principle.

Monthly Expenses for a Digital Nomad

Setting a budget within your means and following it is the foundation for digital nomads. Not planning properly means you could find your travels ending a lot sooner than expected and force you to figure out where next to go.

You must identify variable and fixed monthly expenses to create an accurate budget and stick to it. Many of your expenses will fall under one of these things:

• Clothing
• Internet and mobile phone
• Foods and drinks
• Travel and transportation
• Housing and lodging

You may also have other expenses, depending on how you travel. Thus, fill in the blanks in the list to paint a more accurate picture for yourself. For instance, do you travel with a pet? Then you should add expenses for pet foods and potential vet bills.

When making your budget, begin with the basic expenses and prioritize their insignificance. If you cannot cover all of them, ensure you have enough for obligatory items such as food and housing.

Accommodation for Digital Nomads

With a new generation of people striving to live the modern nomadic life, one in three remote workers prefers to relocate or work abroad. Thus, the accommodation has started to change and the world is adapting to the changes. Here are some of the ever-growing selections of digital nomad accommodation, so that you are completely sorted for where to lay your head anywhere you chose around the world

- **Campervan**

As a remote digital nomad, you have the option to create a DIY van or purchase a prefabricated van. Unfortunately, many prefabricated vans are quite costly. Thus, if you do not wish to spend six figures on a van, you can use the DIY build approach. But if your budget is flexible, it makes more sense to buy a superior, professionally designed campervan. After all, prefabricated vans come with different features and options.

- **Co-living spaces**

Co-living spaces are set to increase and expand with the ever-growing trend of digital nomads becoming popular with the next generation. One benefit of co-living spaces is sharing space with others going through the same experiences and having the same idea as yours.

- **Couchsurfing**

Working on the road and looking for accommodation in a new home every several days may sound time-consuming and tiring, but it can also be rewarding. A whole culture and community of couch surfing have existed for a few years in many locations throughout America, Asia, and Europe.

- **Hostels**

With an air of exploration, like-minded fellow travelers lend their cheap accommodation hostels to digital nomads and their other needs. Many hostels can be seen globally. A basic search will bring you to the one that best suits your requirements.

- **Serviced apartments**

Securing an apartment in a new place is a great feeling, but it comes with other added expenses, such as personal belongings, furniture, appliances, and the internet. As a digital nomad, you wish to move in and get going without getting hung up on those things. That's where serviced apartments come in.

These are apartments kitted out with everything you need from the time you walk through the door. One advantage of serviced apartments is the comfort of moving out anytime you want without added luggage. There's no heavy dinner set to bring out or stressful internet provider you need to negotiate with. Everything is already there from the get-go.

- **Short-term apartments**

When working and traveling around the world as a digital nomad, it can sometimes be difficult to find accommodation that fits your lifestyle. In fact, nineteen percent of new digital nomads mentioned that they find it difficult to find accommodation in new places.

One typical option you can consider for your short-term stay is to rent an apartment on a short-term basis. The benefit of this accommodation option is to feel grounded in your space without any long-term commitments.

Furthermore, you can agree with the landlord about your length of stay, be it a couple of months or a few weeks. Short-term apartments also suggest you don't need to trade your domestic lifestyle while on the road.

With more property owners noticing the potential of housing options for digital nomads, there will be a constant increase in short-term apartments globally. For now, platforms such as Airbnb and Homelike are ideal for finding digital nomad housing.

• Long-term apartments

Digital nomad rentals are often perceived as short-term stays by nature, but there are instances when long-term properties are more necessary. Working from 'home' in your new place and apartment is an excellent way to approach a digital nomad lifestyle.

The benefit of renting long-term accommodation is a sense of long-term security. Having a 1-year lease on an apartment means you no longer need to think about how you will look for accommodation for the months you're in that location.

• Hotels

Hotels are the most expensive option on this list, as you get a private space, access to facilities like Wi-Fi, laundry, hot shower, and often breakfast. Hotels are the most luxurious option as well.

You can use hotel booking platforms such as Expedia to look for and book a hotel for your stay. However, they will not enable you to look for a stay longer than thirty days. Most hotels allow extended stays and provide a discounted rate for people who want to stay longer.

Are you looking for a place to stay longer than a month? Then you must pick a hotel you're interested in. Call the hotel directly and ask if they discount longer stays.

- **Transportation Costs**

Airfare could add up and might be the top cause that could hold a digital nomad back from visiting a place in mind. But that does not have to be the case. Low-cost flights are not difficult to find if you only know where to search and are eager to invest time to save you money.

As for other transportation costs, consider the location of your accommodations and how it could impact your ability to get around.

For instance, when you opt for a cheaper housing option outside the city, you may end up spending money on getting to or from a co-working space. Taxis are relatively cheaper and more convenient now with the rise of Uber and other apps in some countries.

If you are inside the city, you can save money by walking, hiring a bicycle, or using public transportation instead of going by cab or renting a car.

- **Food and Drink Expenses**

Do you love going out to eat? It's not sustainable to do that regularly over a long period, as you'll end up spending a lot of your monthly budget on food.

Are you staying in a certain location for a few weeks or longer? Then why don't you cook at home? Rather than working from a café where you'll end up paying for a snack or drink, allocate your budget to a co-working space with free Wi-Fi or coffee, and as for other beverages, factor in some cash for that if you like a beer or two.

- **Clothing Costs**

If you pack light and travel to various climates, you might need to purchase several clothing items throughout the way. Second-hand and thrift stores are your best friends. Depending on where you are, you might purchase quality bootleg clothes. To keep your bag manageable, you can maintain a "one in, one out" rule. Are you planning on buying a new shirt? Donate the old shirt.

What's more, understand that you might need to get special gear for local weather conditions. Try to have some cash kept away for occasional expenses such as wool socks, rain slickers, or thermal layers.

● **Mobile Phone & Internet Costs**

A reliable internet connection is very important to you as a digital nomad. Luckily, that won't be a separate expense for you. Co-working and housing spaces often include Wi-Fi, or you can find it free in public spaces like coffee shops. As for your mobile phone, you can pay for a mobile plan or a temporary SIM card. And if the internet connection is generous, you will be able to use it to talk or text when you are connected.

Taking your time to run a budget may seem time-consuming, but if sustaining a digital nomad lifestyle over time is your goal, then it's a vital practice. Take the time and crunch all those numbers. It will certainly pay off in the end.

ALL THE GEAR

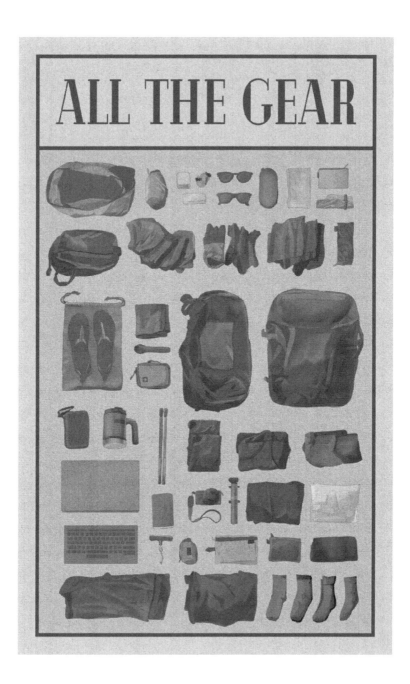

Chapter 7
All the Gear

"Simplify your life. Don't waste the years struggling for things that are unimportant. Don't burden yourself with possessions. Keep your needs and wants simple and enjoy what you have."
Henry David Thoreau

Take a minimalist view of your belongings. Look around your room, your apartment, your house, and think about all that stuff you've got in storage or your friend's house. Do you need it? Have you used your belongings in the last 6 to 12 months?

Packing light for long-term travel can be a huge challenge for digital nomads who bring electronics and tech gear to support their work. Remember this is not about deprivation, you need to be comfortable but it is often surprising to find out how much you need in your day-to-day activities.

The mere mention of the term "packing" could cause most people to sweat or induce stress. Packing abroad as a remote worker or digital nomad during a global health pandemic can be even more challenging. After all, you can fit your entire life into a backpack or suitcase. That's why you need to ensure you bring all the digital nomad essentials or it negatively impacts your long-term life on the road.

As an experienced and seasoned digital nomad, I have learned many things after visiting numerous countries. From what to pack to what I can leave at home; I will share what I think you must consider bringing on the road.

Very often, what you need to survive on the road can be very minimal. Perhaps you only need two or three changes of clothes. You can buy more depending on the climate. Clearly, there are essentials like your passport, your bank account details with app access.

There are online virtual banking services now in many countries, with better exchange rates that can come in handy. You will need your work stuff, your mobile office, a laptop/tablet, and a mobile phone. These days your music, movies, books can all be stored or streamed electronically.

You will need some insurance, often credit cards will provide some level of travel insurance as a perk. So apart from toiletries and somewhere to sleep in the night to keep you warm and some food, you don't need much more, and many nomads will travel like this.

Nomads don't often travel with checked-in baggage, so it can be put into the overhead locker or beneath the seat in front on a flight, train, or coach. Consciously it gives a focus to minimize everything to fit in your bag. If you are traveling you might top up as you travel, but don't top up expensive things so that you can ditch them when you are ready to move on.

Gear for Work

External hard drive

Everyone has cloud storage, right? However, if the internet is poor or as a backup to your cloud storage, it's smart to bring along an external hard drive. Make sure you protect your files too, backup your photos, and have access to them even without an internet connection.

A USB flash drive might do the job for some days or months, but you need to invest in things that could last. These begin at $45, depending on the storage size.

Also, consider your field of work when choosing the flash drive's size. If you work with photos and videos, go for a 4TB flash drive or you can go for a 1TB drive. Whatever the case, pick one that can be locked with a password.

Mobile hotspot

The most important thing for a digital nomad is the internet. After all, that's what enables digital nomads to do their work remotely. Unfortunately, in most cases, nomads are in a scenario where the Wi-Fi service isn't as good as marketed in their workplace or apartment where their adventure brings them. You can prevent disappointment by bringing a mobile hotspot device along with you.

A mobile hotspot is a portable router that works with a SIM card or without a SIM. It has its international packages or daily charge based on your data consumption. You can find these mobile hotspots starting at US$40 depending on the location.

Remember that other brands operate in a predetermined list of countries. Ensure your destinations are on the list before buying.

Noise-canceling headphones

As a digital nomad, you'll find yourself working from airports, coffee shops, or other busy places where it could get noisy. How can you concentrate on your work? It will help if you invest in noise-canceling headphones.

These devices can start from 30 US dollars and will allow you to disengage from the surrounding noise and concentrate on the task at hand. Try to choose noise-canceling headphones with a decent, clear microphone to make calls. With that, you don't need another pair of headphone, as it also saves more space inside your bag.

Portable laptop charger

Digital nomads consider their laptops as their lifeline. That is where you will perform all your work, and you need it charged and accessible at all times. That's when a portable laptop charger comes in handy.

Many models accessible begin from US$79, and you can charge them using a car battery or solar power. Ensure you choose a portable laptop charger that suits your requirements.

It will help if you pick a portable charger, which can be used for both phone and laptop. That will also save you extra space.

All-in-one adapter

There's no doubt that an adapter is our classic travel essential, particularly when moving between continents. You can find several ones on the market with prices beginning from US$8. There are other choices with USB ports for charging your various devices.

When buying an adapter, make sure you pick one that has built-in fuse protection to prevent any damage to your devices in case of fluctuation in current.

Easy Access Items & Accessories

There are other important items you need to bring to your journey. These include the following:

• Glasses for reading in the sun
• Medical certificates
• International driver's license
• Passport along with the needed validity date depending on the country you're visiting
• Wallet which includes your ID, credit cards, some cash, and more
• Diary or Journal to keep your digital nomad life organized while on the road

Clothing

Depending on your interests, hobbies, and the season of your travel destination, your clothing packing list may significantly vary. The goal is to pack like a minimalist, without thinking, *"Gosh, I forgot that,"* only a few hours after your arrival.

Your clothing selections will need to be carefully thought out and applicable for a wide array of events, activities, and places. I will split it into sections:

Miscellaneous Equipment

These are the things that I use and split up in my luggage accordingly.

• First-aid kit – Ensure that your first-aid kit is composed of all the important items like plasters, pain killers, Immodium, anti-inflammatories, Valoid, and more
• Shared toiletries including moisturizer, shampoo, sunblock, toothpaste, toothbrush, etc. Ensure you wrap them in a plastic bag to prevent spillage.

Tips for a Minimalist Packing List

When we think of minimalist, we think free and simple. You should have that mindset when packing your things. The simpler, the freer you will be to get the most of your travel. The less you pack, the less time you will spend picking an outfit, finding things, and rearranging when it is time to repack.

Here are some tips on how you can pack the minimalist style:

- **Use a smaller backpack**

One way to travel light is by using a smaller backpack and using small luggage or backpack of any type results in a few good items. You will be forced to be organized, find things simpler, and you will not be able to purchase unnecessary stuff.

A 40-liter bag or under will enable you to travel with cabin luggage with no worries of being charged extra.

- **Use packing cubes**

Packing cubes are small bags that fit inside your luggage or backpack, and they will change your life. They do not just keep things clean, but they enable you to fit more in your bag. You can use these to sort your clothes and store smaller items that get lost in your bags, such as phone chargers and socks.

- **Pack versatile clothing**

You may have favorite items you wear daily but put that idea aside when packing for your next destination. Packing clothes that could be mixed and matched is key for minimalist backpacking. Additionally, neutral-colored clothes are perfect for this.

That flattering black shirt you have that looks amazing with most bottoms is a better option than the floral top that you can only pair with that pair of jeans.

- **Don't bring the non-essentials**

You may love that big coffee mug you drink out regularly, but there is a good chance you will not need that on your entire trip. Be honest with yourself about the things you will be okay with while discovering a new place. Most likely, you will end up throwing off those things as you go, so you may hold on to them for later or just donate the non-essentials.

Now, it's your turn. It takes time to become a minimalist backpacking pro. Nonetheless, practice makes everything perfect. Later, it will become your second nature to arrange your packing cubs, bring only the essentials, and get creative with mixing and matching your outfits.

All the belongings you don't use or the clothes you don't wear, you can sell them using platforms such as eBay. You can give it away to charity, shops or friends, but if you feel you need your items then hire lock-up storage or talk to relatives to store it in their garage.

Do you really think you think you need those stuff or is it just sentimental? The idea of minimalism complements digital nomadism, making you feel lighter, it will make your life easier because if you know you have to travel tomorrow, you will just have to pick up the bag, throw your stuff in, and off you go. It is also really a lovely feeling, not having to worry about checking in baggage and waiting for baggage on the other end, which may get lost.

If you have ever been on holiday, you may remember that you don't wear half the stuff in the suitcase and you probably would bring more back home. The more space you've got the more you'll be able to fill when coming back.

THE UPSIDES
AND
DOWNSIDES

Chapter 8
The Upsides and Downsides

"Having fun at work is not a diversion from productivity. In fact, it's an essential ingredient to staying loose, open, creative, and solution-oriented. Fun makes for easy lifting. You can have strong ideas, great products, and a brilliant team—but fun (once again) is the grease on the chain that keeps the whole bike rolling."

Life is Good: The Book –Bert Jacobs

It is quite fantastic to work while traveling to different countries. Right? However, being a digital nomad has its pros and cons. it is most surely a dream job. Still, it is difficult and not the lifestyle for everybody.

Therefore, before you begin looking for digital nomad jobs or begging your employer to let you work remotely, take note of the reasons why it is also challenging to become a digital nomad and the benefits of becoming one as well.

The Upsides

Ultimate freedom

The digital nomad lifestyle offers you the freedom you will not get elsewhere. Without normal life's structure, you don't have to go through the stress of most daily things weighing you down. No more worrying about making it work on time, paying for monthly mortgage bills, or having to follow the structure of a traditional working day. Life is as you create it, and your schedule is 100% up to you.

Meet new, awesome people

Traveling across the world and living on the road offers you the opportunity to meet people you would never have met in any other circumstance. Whether through social media groups dedicated to the digital nomad lifestyle or in person as you visit cafes, places of interest, and monuments, the chance to meet someone new is certain.

Do you know that some of the best people are in places that you never would encounter without being a digital nomad?

Get inspiration everywhere you go

The world is surely a big inspirational place, and some of the most hidden, smallest areas are the most interesting. Living your life full of travel and continuous moving shows you will find inspiration no matter where you go.

Additionally, the people you meet, the sites you see, and the places you visit all offer you fulfillment and inspiration that you would not get without living this type of lifestyle.

Continuous travel

Never-ending places to live, never-ending places to see are a major benefit of living a digital nomad life. It also means that you get to travel whenever you wish and stay wherever your heart desires.

The list is endless and exhilarating. The digital nomad lifestyle offers you the chance to feel the world in a way that you have never experienced before. That's a big draw for people seeking to live life to the fullest.

From visiting the ocean to spending a week in the mountains to seeing the most majestic volcanoes, life as a digital nomad offers you the chance to experience the world.

Interesting jobs

One of the advantages of living as a digital nomad is the selection of jobs. The job choices are nearly unlimited and thrilling. The list of what you can do is a massive draw for people wanting to live as one.

Jobs involve marketing, being a full-time blogger, working as a remote writer or freelancer, making and selling your products, and even becoming a voice artist! On top of that, there are many options, and every job is only as exhilarating as the next.

Work whenever and wherever

Ultimately, living a digital nomad life enables you to work whenever and where you wish. Digital nomad jobs do not need you to be in the office or adhere to specific hours. You are left with a schedule that you make and the world as your own office space.

Whether you are on the seaside in your RV, in the mountains, or wish to work from a slowly swinging hammock, the opportunities are endless.

The Downsides

Lack of consistency

You see, life on the road simply indicates very little consistency. It may appear like a good thing at first. It also indicates you don't have any consistency at work and your social life. The continuous inconsistency and change could be a bit straining and challenging to live with unless you are the kind of person who flourishes on change and inconsistency.

Relationships

One of the drawbacks of becoming a digital nomad could be extremely discouraging. Finding and sustaining a relationship while on the road is not that simple unless you travel with someone.

Even then, keeping a relationship with somebody you are traveling with could be complicated with all the stress of living as a digital nomad. Moreover, seeking a new relationship needs a huge amount of effort. It is not simple to convince someone (even yourself) that a long-distance relationship is always worth it.

Missing important milestones

Living life on the road could cause many drawbacks for digital nomads. Missing milestones is one of those challenges. Without living in a permanent place, it is sure to be far away to attend weddings, birthdays, or other special events.

It also suggests you will not be around for other, smaller milestones like your nephew's first steps. It can also be discouraging to miss important milestones in the lives of those people you love and could add to the overall loneliness you feel from life on the road.

Time management and self-reliance

Living as a digital nomad needs a decent handle on time management. With the lack of structure and the freedom you are allotted, it can seem that time management is not something you need to think about.

Nonetheless, time management is very crucial. Finding the ideal balance and schedule to sustain personal care, social life, and work is challenging. It is simple to get lost in your experiences instead of taking care of yourself or getting work done.

Living as a digital nomad could be complex if you do not have self-discipline and powerful time management skills.

Loneliness

A big downside for digital nomads is that life will get quite lonely, particularly traveling independently. You often feel a sense of disconnection from the people you love who reside in another place. It can also be challenging to keep a solid social life while on the road, as well as a feeling of guilt that can arise from living such a lifestyle.

Life as a digital nomad could make for a lot of loneliness, from places where you know no one at all to dead zones without an internet connection.

Burnout

Digital nomadism and remote working have been packaged to prevent burnout in average jobs. However, it still carries the risk. Although, it is in a different form with different triggers. Still, just like in a standard, static job, if you do not handle those triggers properly, you can easily experience the same concerns. You can also experience burnout if you do not handle your time well, separate your social life and work-life, and set boundaries.

Travel becomes a routine

You will most likely become jaded to some level no matter how hard you try. It is extremely challenging not to start taking the travel lifestyle for granted.

After spending a few months or years living on the road, travel might become less special than it once was.

Epilogue

Is Life as Digital Nomad Right for You?

"Do not accept the roles that society foists on you. Re-create yourself by forging a new identity, one that commands attention and never bores the audience."

The 48 Laws of Power – Robert Greene

To sum up, like most big decisions in life, there are many upsides and downsides to becoming a digital nomad. It is not a simple choice to make, but you may find that the pros surely outweigh the cons of becoming one. For the digital nomad and as part of the human condition, one important aspect to consider in this lifestyle is the value of time over money.

Being a digital nomad is not running away into the hills and becoming a hippy. Clearly, money is important, and whilst you don't need to be a millionaire or billionaire, you do need to be focused and often work on yourself to get the freedom of time. You are working towards the life that you feel you should have, "escaping the herd" as the motivational posters suggest - you only have one shot at life.

Moving into digital nomadism is also taking a mental leap, for many it is avoiding being tied down, from the routine of day-to-day living, consuming popular culture and media and in a negative, risk-averse mindset, surrounded by negative people in a job that is hated.

Digital nomadism offers an opportunity to not be a cog in somebody else's machine, it helps you build your own infrastructure and give the opportunity to work for yourself.

Hopefully, this guide helps you understand the realities of becoming a digital nomad. I love being nomadic and feel blessed to work remotely and travel simultaneously. However, only because it is my dream job does not indicate it is ideal for everybody. So, take your time to do your research. Test the water first and take time to understand the downsides of being a digital nomad before leaping!